Color Photo Games

EARLY LITERACY

18 Full–Color Games That Reinforce Essential Early Literacy Skills

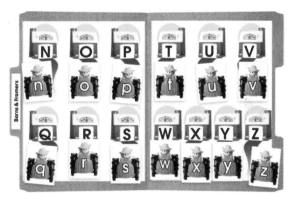

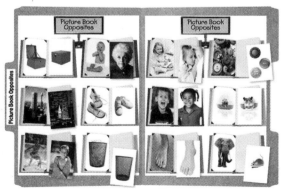

by
Pamela K. Hill

Key Education
An imprint of Carson-Dellosa Publishing LLC
Greensboro, North Carolina

www.keyeducationpublishing.com

CONGRATULATIONS ON YOUR PURCHASE OF A KEY EDUCATION PRODUCT!

The editors at Key Education are former teachers who bring experience, enthusiasm, and quality to each and every product. Thousands of teachers have looked to the staff at Key Education for new and innovative resources to make their work more enjoyable and rewarding. We are committed to developing educational materials that will assist teachers in building a strong and developmentally appropriate curriculum for young children.

PLAN FOR GREAT TEACHING EXPERIENCES WHEN YOU USE EDUCATIONAL MATERIALS FROM KEY EDUCATION PUBLISHING

About the Author

With a BA degree in French and a minor in art history and an MA in museum studies with concentrations in art history and education, Pamela K. Hill worked as an art museum educator before beginning her career in educational publishing. As a product developer and an acquisitions editor, she designed and wrote many posters, games, and other teaching tools for preschool and elementary students and teachers. She also helped authors develop their own teacher resource books. Pamela lives in North Carolina with her husband and two young sons.

Credits

Author: Pamela K. Hill
Project Director: Sherrill B. Flora
Editors: Claude Chalk & Sherrill B. Flora
Cover & Inside Page Design: Annette Hollister-Papp
Cover Photographs: © Shutterstock

Key Education

An imprint of Carson-Dellosa Publishing LLC
PO Box 35665
Greensboro, NC 27425 USA
www.keyeducationpublishing.com

ISBN 978-1-60268-121-7
1-335117784

Contents

Introduction

In any classroom, there are those times when you need a quick way to reinforce essential literacy skills. Is it centers time? Do you have a student who has finished their work early? Is it free choice time? Would you like to send a fun learning activity home? These simple, fun, and engaging games are perfect for all these times. Easy to assemble, fun to play, and designed for individual or small group use, *Color Photo Games: Early Literacy* reinforce essential early literacy skills.

These games are special in a couple ways:
1. They include photographic artwork, so they are developmentally appropriate for young learners.
2. Each game comes with strategies so you can differentiate instruction according to your students' needs.

Assembly Tips for all Games

Supplies you will need:
- ✦ colorful file folders, shirt boxes with lids (dimensions at least 11" x 17"), or 11" x 17" poster board
- ✦ scissors
- ✦ white glue or glue stick
- ✦ self-sealing plastic bags
- ✦ laminator and laminating film or self-stick plastic sheets
- ✦ stapler
- ✦ pen

See specific game assembly directions on the introduction page of each game.

Ideas for using *Color Photo Games: Early Literacy*:
- ✦ Place games that support your curriculum in your learning centers.
- ✦ Give individual games to students at their seats for targeted skill practice.
- ✦ Send file folder games home for practice with family.
- ✦ Demonstrate each game to your students before they use it individually or in small groups.

Correlations to the Standards

This book supports the recommended teaching practices outlined in the NAEYC/IRA position statement *Learning to Read and Write: Developmentally Appropriate Practices for Young Children* and many domain element examples in *The Head Start Child Development and Early Learning Framework*.

───── **NAEYC/IRA Position Statement** *Learning to Read and Write: Developmentally Appropriate Practices for Young Children* ─────

The activities in this book support the following recommended teaching practices for Preschool students:

1. **Teachers promote the development of phonemic awareness through appropriate songs, finger plays, games, poems, and stories.** Many of the games in *Color Photo Games: Early Literacy* promote the development of phonemic awareness by supporting picture/sound correspondence, initial letter/sound correspondence, and rhyme recognition.
2. **Teachers provide opportunities for children to participate in literacy play, incorporating both reading and writing.** *Color Photo Games: Early Literacy* contains 18 literacy games that incorporates reading for students.
3. **Teachers provide experiences and materials that help children expand their vocabularies.** The games in *Color Photo Games: Early Literacy* support vocabulary development by presenting pictures of a wide variety of objects that students must name to play the games.

The activities in this book support the following recommended teaching practices for Kindergarten and Primary students:

1. **Teachers read to children daily and provide opportunities for students to independently read both fiction and nonfiction texts.** Students must read letters and pictures to play the games in *Color Photo Games: Early Literacy*. They also read the directions for the games once they are able.
2. **Teachers provide balanced literacy instruction that incorporates systematic phonics instruction along with meaningful reading and writing activities.** *Color Photo Games: Early Literacy* includes games that support phonemic awareness and early phonics.
3. **Teachers provide opportunities for children to work in small groups.** Teachers can use the games in *Color Photo Games: Early Literacy* with small groups.
4. **Teachers provide challenging instruction that expands children's knowledge of their world and expands vocabulary.** The games in *Color Photo Games: Early Literacy* support vocabulary development by presenting pictures of a wide variety of objects that students must name to play the games.
5. **Teachers adapt teaching strategies based on the individual needs of a child.** *Color Photo Games: Early Literacy* includes strategies for adapting the games to different student needs.

───────── *The Head Start Child Development and Early Learning Framework* ─────────
**U. S. Department of Health and Human Services, Administration on Children, Youth and Families/Head Start Bureau.
The Head Start Child Development and Early Learning Framework. Washington, D.C.**

Activities in this book support the following examples in the Head Start Child Outcomes Framework:

Physical Development & Health: Fine Motor Skills
- Develops hand strength and dexterity.
- Manipulates a range of objects, such as blocks or books.

Logic & Reasoning: Reasoning & Problem Solving
- Classifies, compares, and contrasts objects, events, and experiences.

Literacy Knowledge & Skills: Phonological Awareness
- Identifies and discriminates between separate syllables in words.
- Identifies and discriminates between sounds and phonemes in language, such as attention to beginning and ending sounds of words and recognition that different words begin or end with the same sound.

Literacy Knowledge & Skills: Alphabet Knowledge
- Recognizes that the letters of the alphabet are a special category of visual graphics that can be individually named.
- Recognizes that letters of the alphabet have distinct sound(s) associated with them.
- Attends to the beginning letters and sounds in familiar words.
- Identifies letters and associates correct sounds with letters.

Literacy Knowledge & Skills: Print Concepts & Conventions
- Recognizes print in everyday life, such as numbers, letters, one's name, words, and familiar logos and sounds.

Game 1:
Same and Different

Skill: Visual discrimination

Preparation and Assembly:

1. **Remove the game materials.** Carefully remove the "Same and Different" game materials found on pages 5–16.

2. **Make the game board.** Glue the two folder game pages (pages 7 and 9) to the inside of a file folder, shirt box, or on poster board.

3. **Game directions.** Cut out the game directions (below) and glue them to the front of the file folder, on the outside of the shirt box, or on the edge of the poster board.

4. **Two game title labels.** Glue one game title label to the file folder tab, on the outside of the shirt box, or on the poster board, and then laminate for durability.

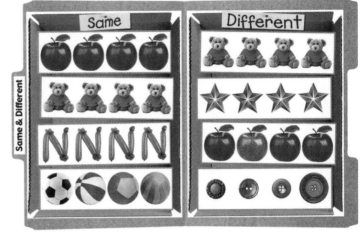

5. **Self-sealing plastic storage bag.** Tape the second game title label on the self-sealing plastic bag and then staple or tape the bag to the front of the file folder, top of the shirt box, or on the edge of the poster board.

6. **Game cards.** Cut out the game cards found on pages 11 to 15 and laminate for durability. Place the cards in the self-sealing plastic bag. Your game is now ready to play!

Game Objective: The objective is for the child to correctly place the game cards into the "same" box or the "different" box.

To Play the Game: Talk about the concept of "same" and "different." Discuss that the pictures on the cards might all be the same color, the same shape, or the same size. Place the cards face-up in a pile. A child draws the top card, looks at it and places it into one of the two game board boxes.

To Modify the Game for Struggling Learners: Show the game cards to the child before playing the game. Talk about the pictures on the cards and decide together if the objects are the "same" or if one of the objects on the card is "different." The child can play the game independently once he is able to explain how the objects on the cards are the "same" or how the objects are "different."

Self-Checking: The back of the game cards will show the child which box the card belongs. If it is the "same" the word "same" will be on the card back. If it is different, the word "different" and a picture of the different object will be on the card back.

Same and Different

Directions: Look at the pictures on a game card.

If all the pictures are the same, put the card in the "Same" box.

If one of the pictures is different, put the card in the "Different" box.

Same & Different

Same & Different

(This page was purposely left blank.)

Same

(Same and Different Folder Left-Side)

(This page was purposely left blank.)

Different

(This page was purposely left blank.)

Same

Different

Same

Different

-12-

Same

Different

Different

Same

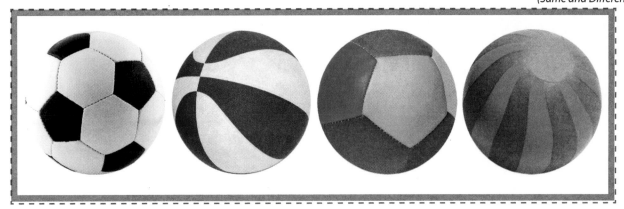

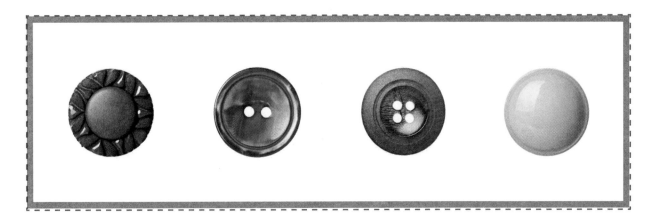

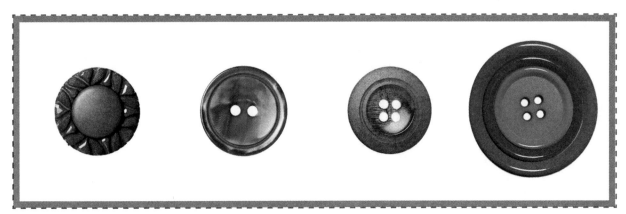

Same

Different

Same

Different

Game 2:
It's in the Bag!

Skill: Things that go together/classification

Preparation and Assembly

1. **Remove the game materials.** Carefully remove the "It's in the Bag!" game materials found on pages 17–24.
2. **Make the game board.** Glue the two folder game pages (pages 19 and 21) to the inside of a file folder, shirt box, or on poster board.
3. **Game directions.** Cut out the game directions (below) and glue them to the front of the file folder, on the outside of the shirt box, or on the edge of the poster board.
4. **Two game title labels.** Glue one game title label to the file folder tab, on the outside of the shirt box, or on the poster board, and then laminate for durability.
5. **Self-sealing plastic storage bag.** Tape the second game title label on the self-sealing plastic bag and then staple or tape the bag to the front of the file folder, top of the shirt box, or on the edge of the poster board.
6. **Game cards.** Cut out the game cards found on page 23 and laminate for durability. Place the cards in the self-sealing plastic bag. Your game is now ready to play!

Game Objective: The objective is for the child to match two pictures of items that go-together.

To Play the Game: Place the game cards in a pile face-up. The child draws the top card, says the name of the item pictured on the card, and then places the card in its matching "go-together" bag. Ask the child to explain why he thinks the two items "go-together."

To Modify the Game for Struggling Learners: Show the child the game board. Talk about the pictures on each of the bags. Ask the child if he can come up with other items that could "go-together" with the pictures on the bags. For example, look at the tennis shoes on the blue bag. Ask the child to name things that could go with the tennis shoes. The child might respond with boots, slippers, socks, or shoe laces. His answers will let you know how much he is understanding the "go-together" concept.

Self-Checking: The correct game board bag is pictured on the back of each game card. For example, the back of the pencils game card shows the green bag, which has the picture of the paper.

It's in the Bag!

Directions: Take a picture card from the plastic bag.

Find the bag that has something that goes with that picture card on it.

Put the picture card on the matching bag.

It's in the Bag!

It's in the Bag

(This page was purposely left blank.)

It's In The Bag

(It's in the Bag! Folder Left-Side)

(This page was purposely left blank.)

It's In The Bag

(It's in the Bag! Folder Right-Side)

(This page was purposely left blank.)

Things That Go Toether Key:

paper/pencils	toothbrush/toothpaste
dog/dog food	milk/cookies
comb/brush	hammer/nail
shoes/socks	bed/pillow

Game 3:
Picture Book Opposites

Skill: Matching opposite pictures

Preparation and Assembly

1. **Remove the game materials.** Carefully remove the "Picture Book Opposites" game materials found on pages 25–32.
2. **Make the game board.** Glue the two folder game pages (pages 27 and 29) to the inside of a file folder, shirt box, or on poster board.
3. **Game directions.** Cut out the game directions (below) and glue them to the front of the file folder, on the outside of the shirt box, or on the edge of the poster board.
4. **Two game title labels.** Glue one game title label to the file folder tab, on the outside of the shirt box, or on the poster board, and then laminate for durability.

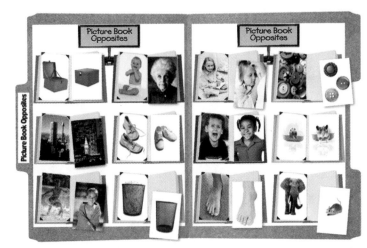

5. **Self-sealing plastic storage bag.** Tape the second game title label on the self-sealing plastic bag and then staple or tape the bag to the front of the file folder, top of the shirt box, or on the edge of the poster board.
6. **Game cards.** Cut out the game cards found on page 31 and laminate for durability. Place the cards in the self-sealing plastic bag. Your game is now ready to play!

Game Objective: The objective is for the child to correctly place each opposite game card next to its correct opposite on the game board. For example, the "closed" box would go on book 1 next to the "open" box.

To Play the Game: Place the game cards in a pile face-up. The child draws the top card, says the name of the item pictured on the card, and then places the card next to its matching opposite. Ask the child to explain why he thinks the two items are opposites.

To Modify the Game for Struggling Learners: The concept of "opposites" can be difficult for some children. Before playing the game make sure the children have some understanding of the concept. Use real items at first and then move on to discuss picture card opposites. Play the game together. Hold up one card for example, and say " I have a little mouse. What picture on the board shows the opposite of *little*?"

Self-Checking: The back of each game card is labeled with that card's correct location on the game board. For example, the game card with "night" has BOOK 3 on its back—so it would go next to the "day" picture on Book 3.

Picture Book Opposites

Directions: Look at the picture on a book. Say the word.

Find a picture that means the opposite from the picture in the book.

Put it on the other page of the book.

Picture Book Opposites

Picture Book Opposites

(This page was purposely left blank.)

-26-

Picture Book Opposites

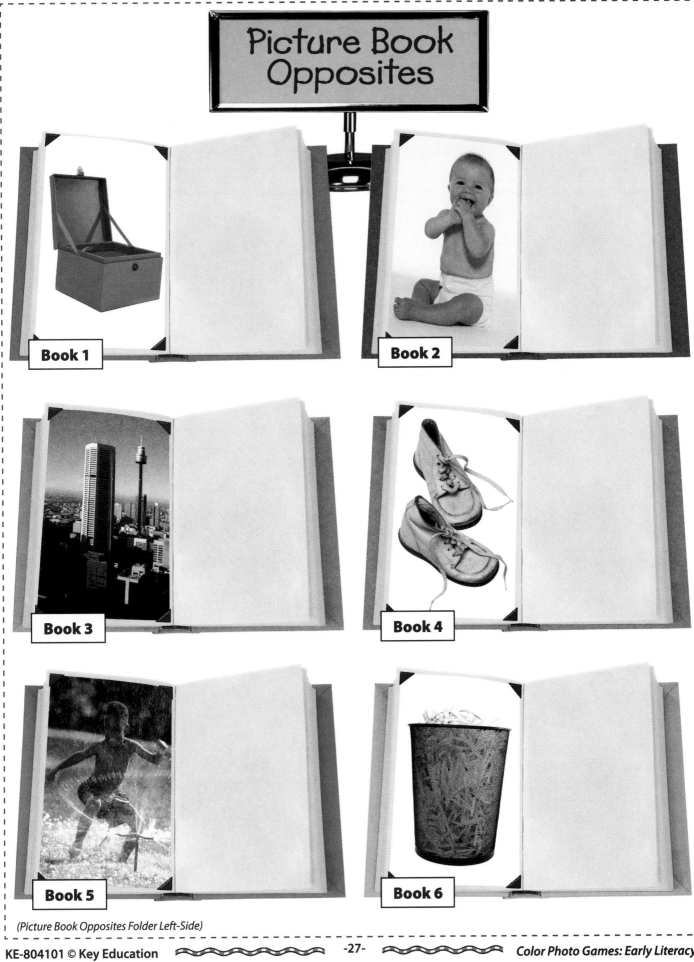

Book 1

Book 2

Book 3

Book 4

Book 5

Book 6

(Picture Book Opposites Folder Left-Side)

(This page was purposely left blank.)

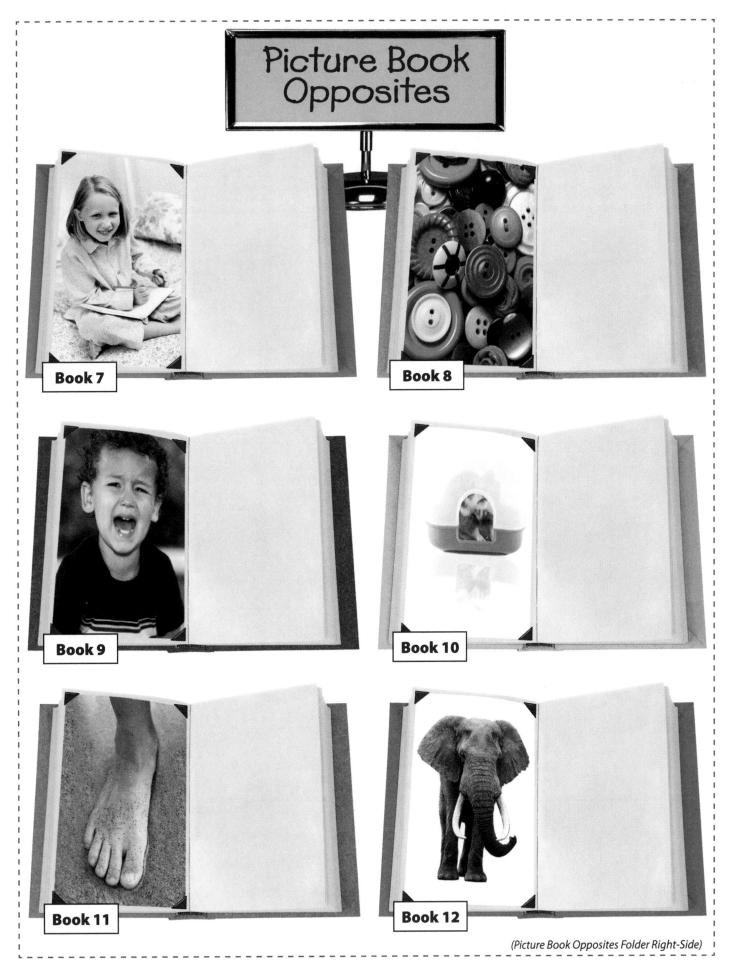

Picture Book Opposites

Book 7

Book 8

Book 9

Book 10

Book 11

Book 12

(This page was purposely left blank.)

Opposites Key:
Book 1: open/closed
Book 2: young/old
Book 3: day/night
Book 4: old/new
Book 5: wet/dry
Book 6: full/empty
Book 7: awake/asleep
Book 8: many/few
Book 9: sad/happy
Book 10: in/out
Book 11: clean/dirty
Book 12: big/little

| Book 7 | Book 1 | Book 10 | Book 8 |

| Book 4 | Book 9 | Book 6 | Book 2 |

| Book 3 | Book 12 | Book 5 | Book 11 |

Game 4:
Hauling Rhymes

Skill: Matching rhyming pictures

Preparation and Assembly

1. **Remove the game materials.** Carefully remove the "Hauling Rhymes" game materials found on pages 33–40.
2. **Make the game board.** Glue the two folder game pages (pages 35 and 37) to the inside of a file folder, shirt box, or on poster board.
3. **Game directions.** Cut out the game directions (below) and glue them to the front of the file folder, on the outside of the shirt box, or on the edge of the poster board.
4. **Two game title labels.** Glue one game title label to the file folder tab, on the outside of the shirt box, or on the poster board, and then laminate for durability.

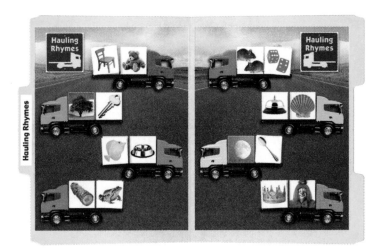

5. **Self-sealing plastic storage bag.** Tape the second game title label on the self-sealing plastic bag and then staple or tape the bag to the front of the file folder, top of the shirt box, or on the edge of the poster board.
6. **Game cards.** Cut out the game cards found on page 39 and laminate for durability. Place the cards in the self-sealing plastic bag. Your game is now ready to play!

Game Objective: The objective is to match each game card to its "rhyme" truck.

To Play the Game: Place the game cards in a pile face-up. The child draws the top card, says the name of the item pictured on the card, and then places the card on the truck that has its matching "rhyme."

To Modify the Game for Struggling Learners: Learning to rhyme is essential for phonemic awareness and difficult for many children. For children struggling with learning how to rhyme, provide only 2 choices. For example, Put two cards next to a truck— one rhyming card and one card that does not rhyme. Ask the child to say the name of the item on the truck, and then say the names of the pictures on the two cards. Fewer choices will not be as overwhelming. Say the words slowly emphasizing the rhymes.

Self-Checking: On the back of each game card is a picture of the correct truck. For example, the back of the "spoon" game card is a picture of the white truck, where the picture of the "moon" can be found.

Hauling Rhymes

Directions: Look at the picture on the truck. Say the word.

Find a picture that rhymes.

Put it in the back of the matching truck.

Hauling Rhymes

Hauling Rhymes

(This page was purposely left blank.)

-35-

(This page was purposely left blank.)

(Hauling Rhymes Folder Right-Side)

(This page was purposely left blank.)

Rhyme Key:

mice/dice	bear/chair
bell/shell	tree/key
moon/spoon	dish/fish
clown/crown	log/frog

Game 5:
Rhyming Houses

Skill: Matching rhyming pictures

Preparation and Assembly

1. **Remove the game materials.** Carefully remove the "Rhyming Houses" game materials found on pages 41–48.
2. **Make the game board.** Glue the two folder game pages (pages 43 and 45) to the inside of a file folder, shirt box, or on poster board.
3. **Game directions.** Cut out the game directions (below) and glue them to the front of the file folder, on the outside of the shirt box, or on the edge of the poster board.
4. **Two game title labels.** Glue one game title label to the file folder tab, on the outside of the shirt box, or on the poster board, and then laminate for durability.
5. **Self-sealing plastic storage bag.** Tape the second game title label on the self-sealing plastic bag and then staple or tape the bag to the front of the file folder, top of the shirt box, or on the edge of the poster board.
6. **Game cards.** Cut out the game cards found on page 47 and laminate for durability. Place the cards in the self-sealing plastic bag. Your game is now ready to play!

Game Objective: The objective is for the child to find the four windows that rhyme with the picture on the each of the house's doors.

To Play the Game: Place the game cards in a pile face-up. The child draws the top card, says the name of the item pictured on the card, and then decides which house has the door that rhymes with the game card. Four children can play—each child choosing a house. The children take turns drawing cards until they have placed a card on all 4 windows of their house. If a card is drawn that is not a match it should be placed on the bottom of the pile.

To Modify the Game for Struggling Learners: Play with only two houses (half the game board) and only eight of the game cards. The child will draw a card and will only have to decide which of the two houses rhymes with the game card drawn.

Self-Checking: Each house is a different color—red, blue, orange, and yellow. The back of each game card has a solid color indicating which house the card goes to. For example, the card with the "top" has an orange back, indicating that "top" rhymes with the "mop" on the orange house.

Rhyming Houses

Directions: Look at the picture on the house door. Say the word.

Find four picture cards that rhyme with it.

Put them in the house's windows.

Rhyming Houses

Rhyming Houses

(This page was purposely left blank.)

House Rhyming

(Rhyming Houses Folder Left-Side)

(This page was purposely left blank.)

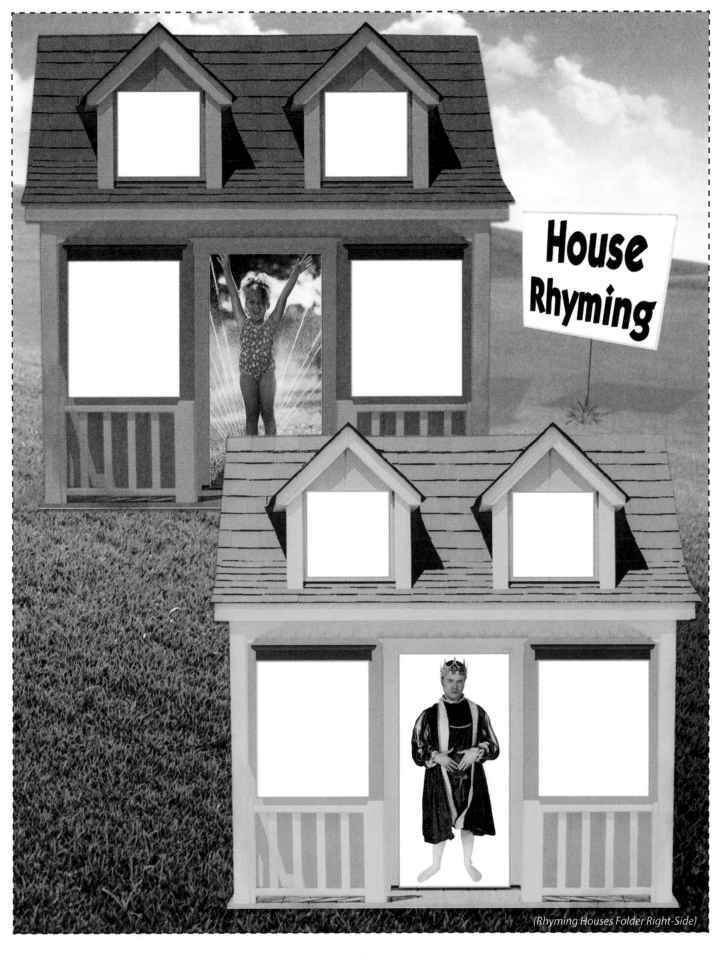

House Rhyming

(Rhyming Houses Folder Right-Side)

(This page was purposely left blank.)

Rhyme Picture Key:
Red House: cat on door, bat, hat, mat, rat
Blue House: mop on door, cop, pop, stop, top
Purple House: wet on door, jet, net, pet, vet
Orange House: king on door, ring, sing, string, wing

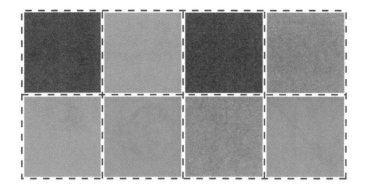

Game 6:
Rhyme Garden

Skill: Sorting rhyming and non-rhyming pairs

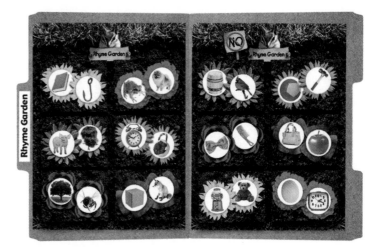

Preparation and Assembly
1. **Remove the game materials.** Carefully remove the "Rhyme Garden" game materials found on pages 49–60.
2. **Make the game board.** Glue the two folder game pages (pages 51 and 53) to the inside of a file folder, shirt box, or on poster board.
3. **Game directions.** Cut out the game directions (below) and glue them to the front of the file folder, on the outside of the shirt box, or on the edge of the poster board.
4. **Two game title labels.** Glue one game title label to the file folder tab, on the outside of the shirt box, or on the poster board, and then laminate for durability.
5. **Self-sealing plastic storage bag.** Tape the second game title label on the self-sealing plastic bag and then staple or tape the bag to the front of the file folder, top of the shirt box, or on the edge of the poster board.
6. **Game cards.** Cut out the game cards found on pages 55 to 60 and laminate for durability. Place the cards in the self-sealing plastic bag. Your game is now ready to play!

Game Objective: The objective is for the child to correctly place the nine game cards with rhyming pairs on the "Rhyme Garden" and place the nine game cards with pictures that DO NOT rhyme on the "No Rhyme Garden."

To Play the Game: Place the game cards in a pile face-up. The child draws the top card, says the name of the two item pictured on the card, and then decides if the two pictures rhyme (and then place the picture on the "Rhyme Garden") or that the pictures do not rhyme (and then place the picture on the "No Rhyme Garden").

To Modify the Game for Struggling Learners: Hearing the subtle differences in phonemes can be difficult. Go through all the cards with the child before playing the game so the child can practice hearing the "rhyming" sounds. Play the game together, slowly saying the words and emphasizing the phonemes. Using a play phone to accentuate the sounds heard can also be beneficial.

Self-Checking: There is a sign on the back of each card. If the card has two pictures that rhyme, the sign with say "Rhyme Garden." If the card has pictures that do not rhyme, the sign will say "No Rhyme Garden."

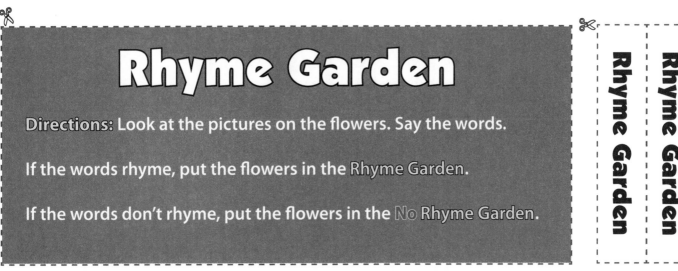

Rhyme Garden

Directions: Look at the pictures on the flowers. Say the words.

If the words rhyme, put the flowers in the Rhyme Garden.

If the words don't rhyme, put the flowers in the No Rhyme Garden.

Rhyme Garden

Rhyme Garden

(This page was purposely left blank.)

Rhyme Garden

(Rhyme Garden Folder Left-Side)

(This page was purposely left blank.)

(Rhyme Garden Folder Right-Side)

(This page was purposely left blank.)

Page 55 Rhyme Key: book/hook, pig/wig, tree/bee, frog/dog, clock/lock, box/fox

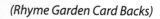

Page 57 Rhyme Card Key: house/mouse, duck/truck, pen/hen, balloon/nail, flower/bus, house/pillow

Page 59 Rhyme Key: egg/clock, ball/hammer, purse/apple, gumball machine/bear, barrel/bird, bow/comb

Game 7:
Syllable Space Stations

Skill: Sorting pictures by the number of syllables

Preparation and Assembly

1. **Remove the game materials.** Carefully remove the "Syllable Space Stations" game materials found on pages 61–68.
2. **Make the game board.** Glue the two folder game pages (pages 63 and 65) to the inside of a file folder, shirt box, or on poster board.
3. **Game directions.** Cut out the game directions (below) and glue them to the front of the file folder, on the outside of the shirt box, or on the edge of the poster board.
4. **Two game title labels.** Glue one game title label to the file folder tab, on the outside of the shirt box, or on the poster board, and then laminate for durability.
5. **Self-sealing plastic storage bag.** Tape the second game title label on the self-sealing plastic bag and then staple or tape the bag to the front of the file folder, top of the shirt box, or on the edge of the poster board.
6. **Game cards.** Cut out the game cards found on page 67 and laminate for durability. Place the cards in the self-sealing plastic bag. Your game is now ready to play!

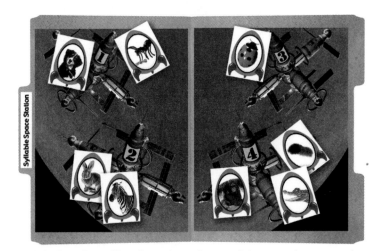

Game Objective: The objective is for the child to place the game cards onto the correct space station by determining how many syllables are in the word pictured on the game card. For example, ant (one syllable) would be placed on space station "one." Ladybug (three syllables) would be placed on space station "three."

To Play the Game: Place the game cards in a pile face-up. The child draws the top card, says the name of the item pictured on the card, and claps for each syllable. He then places the card on the correct space station.

To Modify the Game for Struggling Learners: Be sure that the child says the word and can accurately clap out the syllables. The child must be able to clap and count out the syllables in order to successfully play this game. For children just learning about syllables, use only half the game board, allowing the children to only choose between one and two syllable words. Add additional space stations as the children can count up to four syllables.

Self-Checking: The back of each game card will show the child the numeral of the correct space station.

Syllable Space Stations

Directions: Take a space ship from the pile. Look at the picture and say its name.

Clap and count how many syllables (word parts) the name has.

Put the space ship next to the space station with that number on it.

Syllable Space Stations

Syllable Space Stations

(This page was purposely left blank.)

SYLLABLE SPACE STATIONS

(Syllable Space Stations Folder Left-Side)

(This page was purposely left blank.)

(Syllable Space Stations Folder Right-Side)

(This page was purposely left blank.)

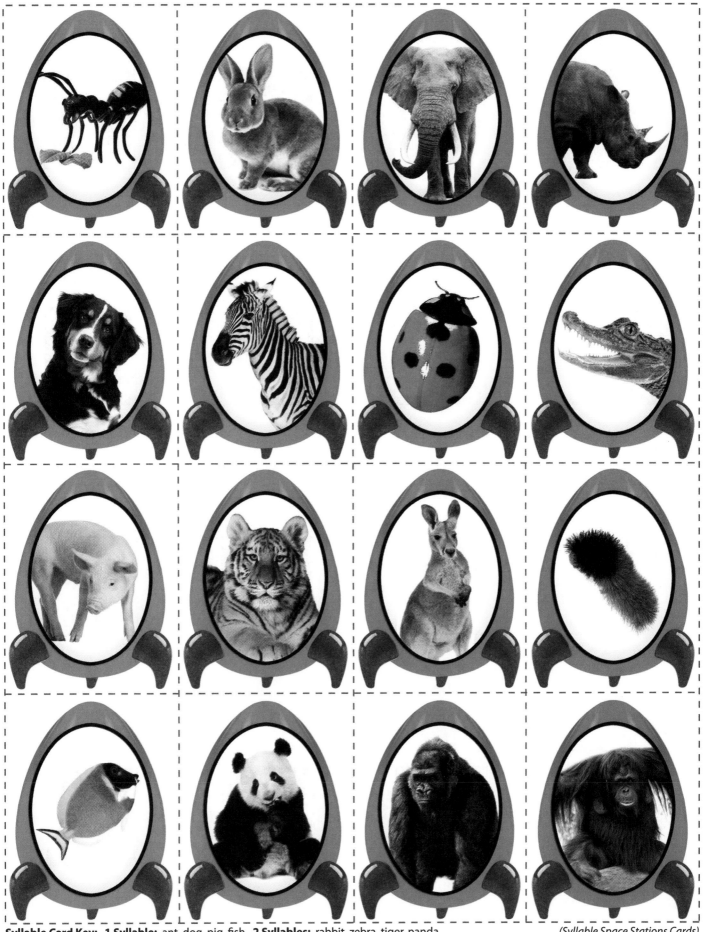

4	3	2	1
4	3	2	1
4	3	2	1
4	3	2	1

Game 8:
Barns and Tractors, A-M

Skill: Matching uppercase and lowercase letters, A-M

Preparation and Assembly

1. **Remove the game materials.** Carefully remove the "Barns and Tractors, A–M" game materials found on pages 69–76.
2. **Make the game board.** Glue the two folder game pages (pages 71 and 73) to the inside of a file folder, shirt box, or on poster board.
3. **Game directions.** Cut out the game directions (below) and glue them to the front of the file folder, on the outside of the shirt box, or on the edge of the poster board.
4. **Two game title labels.** Glue one game title label to the file folder tab, on the outside of the shirt box, or on the poster board, and then laminate for durability.
5. **Self-sealing plastic storage bag.** Tape the second game title label on the self-sealing plastic bag and then staple or tape the bag to the front of the file folder, top of the shirt box, or on the edge of the poster board.
6. **Game cards.** Cut out the game cards found on page 75 and laminate for durability. Place the cards in the self-sealing plastic bag. Your game is now ready to play!

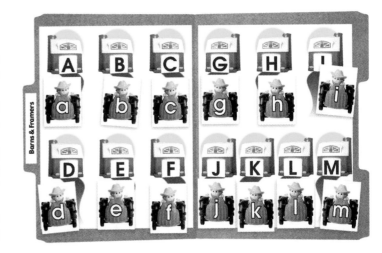

Game Objective: The objective is for the child to match the lowercase letters (tractors) to the uppercase letters (barns).

To Play the Game: Place the game cards in a pile face-up. The child draws the top card and says the name of the lowercase letter on the card, and then places the card under the barn that has the corresponding uppercase letter.

To Modify the Game for Struggling Learners: The alphabet barns on the game board pages are in alphabetical order (which is a great way to begin to learn how to alphabetize and match uppercase to lowercase letters. Although to make the game more of a challenge, you can cut apart the barns and glue them to the game board in random order. It is also fun to combine "Barns and Tractors A-M" with "Barns and Tractors N-Z," so the entire alphabet can be used as one game.

Self-Checking: The correct uppercase letter is printed on the back of each of the Tractor game cards.

Barns and Tractors (A-M)

Directions: Look at the lowercase letter on the card. Say its name.

Find the barn with the uppercase letter that matches.

Put the tractor card below the matching barn.

Barns and Tractors

Barns and Tractors

(This page was purposely left blank.)

Barns and Tractors (A-M)

(This page was purposely left blank.)

(This page was purposely left blank.)

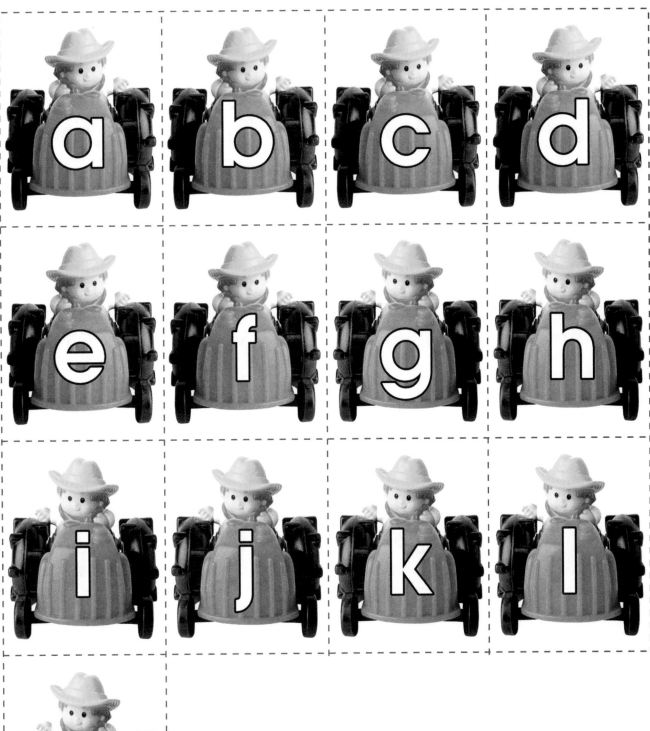

D	C	B	A
H	G	F	E
L	K	J	I
			M

Skill: Matching uppercase and lowercase letters, N-Z

Preparation and Assembly

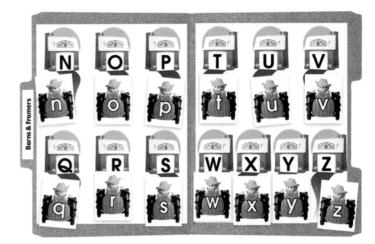

1. **Remove the game materials.** Carefully remove the "Barns and Tractors, N–Z" game materials found on pages 77–84.
2. **Make the game board.** Glue the two folder game pages (pages 79 and 81) to the inside of a file folder, shirt box, or on poster board.
3. **Game directions.** Cut out the game directions (below) and glue them to the front of the file folder, on the outside of the shirt box, or on the edge of the poster board.
4. **Two game title labels.** Glue one game title label to the file folder tab, on the outside of the shirt box, or on the poster board, and then laminate for durability.
5. **Self-sealing plastic storage bag.** Tape the second game title label on the self-sealing plastic bag and then staple or tape the bag to the front of the file folder, top of the shirt box, or on the edge of the poster board.
6. **Game cards.** Cut out the game cards found on page 83 and laminate for durability. Place the cards in the self-sealing plastic bag. Your game is now ready to play!

Game Objective: The objective is for the child to match the lowercase letters (tractors) to the uppercase letters (barns).

To Play the Game: Place the game cards in a pile face-up. The child draws the top card and says the name of the lowercase letter on the card, and then places the card under the barn that has the corresponding uppercase letter.

To Modify the Game for Struggling Learners: The alphabet barns on the game board pages are in alphabetical order (which is a great way to begin to learn how to alphabetize and match uppercase to lowercase letters. Although to make the game more of a challenge, you can cut apart the barns and glue them to the game board in random order. It is also fun to combine "Barns and Tractors A-N" with "Barns and Tractors N-Z," so the entire alphabet can be used as one game.

Self-Checking: The correct uppercase letter is printed on the back of each of the Tractor game cards.

Barns and Tractors (N-Z)

Directions: Look at the lowercase letter on the card. Say its name.

Find the barn with the uppercase letter that matches.

Put the tractor card below the matching barn.

Barns and Tractors

Barns and Tractors

(This page was purposely left blank.)

Barns and Tractors (N-Z)

(Barns and Tractors Folder Left-Side)

(This page was purposely left blank.)

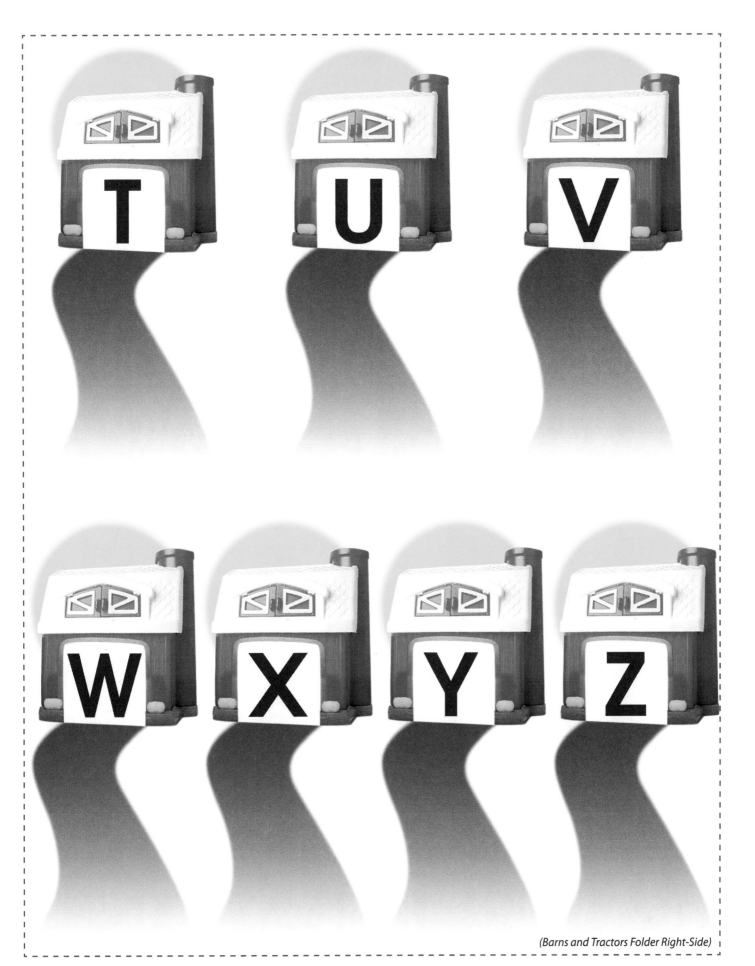

(This page was purposely left blank.)

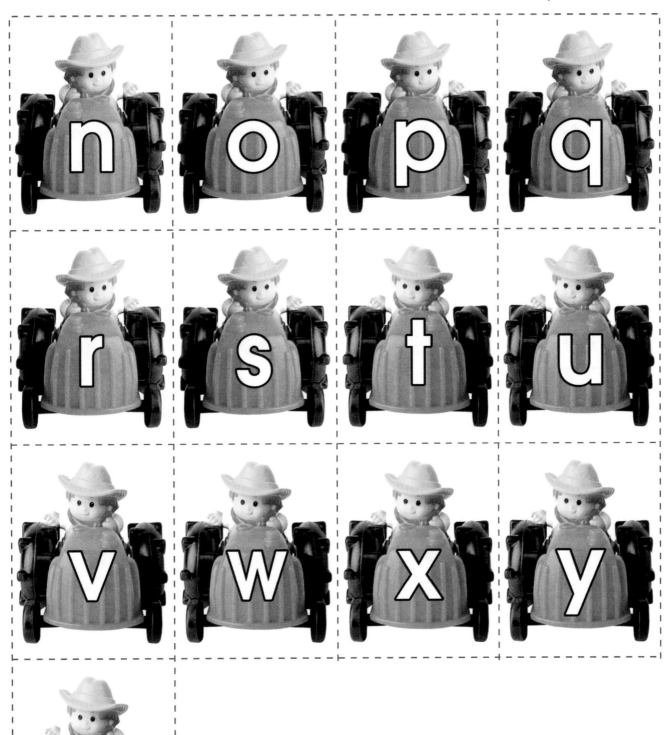

Q	P	O	N
U	T	S	R
Y	X	W	V
			Z

Game 10:
Beginning Sound Buses

Skill: Sorting initial sound pictures (b, c, m, s)

Preparation and Assembly

1. **Remove the game materials.** Carefully remove the "Beginning Sound Buses" game materials found on pages 85–92.
2. **Make the game board.** Glue the two folder game pages (pages 87 and 89) to the inside of a file folder, shirt box, or on poster board.
3. **Game directions.** Cut out the game directions (below) and glue them to the front of the file folder, on the outside of the shirt box, or on the edge of the poster board.
4. **Two game title labels.** Glue one game title label to the file folder tab, on the outside of the shirt box, or on the poster board, and then laminate for durability.
5. **Self-sealing plastic storage bag.** Tape the second game title label on the self-sealing plastic bag and then staple or tape the bag to the front of the file folder, top of the shirt box, or on the edge of the poster board.
6. **Game cards.** Cut out the game cards found on page 91 and laminate for durability. Place the cards in the self-sealing plastic bag. Your game is now ready to play!

Game Objective: The objective is for the child to correctly match game cards with pictures representing phonemes /b/ /c/ /m/ /s/ onto the windows of a school bus that has a picture with the "same" sound.

To Play the Game: Place the game cards in a pile face-up. The child draws the top card, says the name of the item pictured on the card, and then places the card on the window of the school bus that has a picture that begins with the same sound.

To Modify the Game for Struggling Learners: Learning to identify beginning sounds is difficult for many children. For children struggling with matching initial phonemes, provide only two choices. For example, put two cards next to a school bus—one card with the same beginning sound as the picture on the bus and the other card with a different beginning sound. Ask the child to say the name of the item on the card slowly, and then say the name of the picture on the bus. Saying the words slowly will emphasize the beginning sound.

Self-Checking: On the back of the game cards the child wll see the picture on the door of the correct school bus.

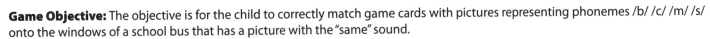

Beginning Sound Buses
(b, c, m, s)

Directions: Look at the picture on the bus. Say the word.

Find a picture card that starts with the same sound. Put it on the window of the bus.

Beginning Sound Buses

Beginning Sound Buses

(This page was purposely left blank.)

Beginning Sound Buses

(Beginning Sound Buses Folder Left-Side)

(This page was purposely left blank.)

(Beginning Sound Buses Folder Right Side)

(This page was purposely left blank.)

Beginning Sound Picture Key:
Basketball Bus: bike, bird, butterfly
Mitten Bus: mirror, mop, mouse
Cake Bus: car, carrot, cat
Sandwich Bus: seal, sink, sun

Game 11:
Beginning Sound Balloons

Skill: Sorting initial sound pictures (f, g, l, t)

Preparation and Assembly

1. **Remove the game materials.** Carefully remove the "Beginning Sound Balloons" game materials found on pages 93–100.
2. **Make the game board.** Glue the two folder game pages (pages 95 and 97) to the inside of a file folder, shirt box, or on poster board.
3. **Game directions.** Cut out the game directions (below) and glue them to the front of the file folder, on the outside of the shirt box, or on the edge of the poster board.
4. **Two game title labels.** Glue one game title label to the file folder tab, on the outside of the shirt box, or on the poster board, and then laminate for durability.
5. **Self-sealing plastic storage bag.** Tape the second game title label on the self-sealing plastic bag and then staple or tape the bag to the front of the file folder, top of the shirt box, or on the edge of the poster board.
6. **Game cards.** Cut out the game cards found on page 99 and laminate for durability. Place the cards in the self-sealing plastic bag. Your game is now ready to play!

Game Objective: The objective is for the child to correctly match balloon game cards with pictures representing phonemes /f/ /g/ /l/ /t/ with the balloons held by the clowns that have the "same" beginning sound.

To Play the Game: Place the game cards in a pile face-up. The child draws the top card, says the name of the picture on the balloon card, and then finds the clown that is holding a balloon with the same sound as the drawn card. Put the card on a space by the balloon with the matching sound.

To Modify the Game for Struggling Learners: For children struggling with learning how to identify beginning sounds, use only half the game board. The children will only have to choose between two different beginning sounds.

Self-Checking: On the back of each of the game cards the child will see the picture on the balloon held by the correct clown.

Beginning Sound Balloons (f, g, l, t)

Directions: Draw a balloon card. Say its name.

Find the clown that is holding a balloon with the same sound as the drawn card.

Put your card on a space by the balloon with the matching sound.

Beginning Sound Balloons

Beginning Sound Balloons

(This page was purposely left blank.)

Beginning Sound Balloons

(Beginning Sound Balloons Folder Left-Side)

(This page was purposely left blank.)

(Beginning Sound Balloons
Folder Right-Side)

(This page was purposely left blank.)

Beginning Sound Picture Key: **"G" Pictures:** gorilla, gifts, goose   **"L" Pictures:** ladder, lamp, lobster
     "T " Pictures: top, table, television   **"F" Pictures:** five, feather, football

Game 12:
Bubblegum Sounds

Skill: Sorting initial sound pictures (d, h, n, w, z)

Preparation and Assembly

1. **Remove the game materials.** Carefully remove the "Bubblegum Sounds" game materials found on pages 101–108.
2. **Make the game board.** Glue the two folder game pages (pages 103 and 105) to the inside of a file folder, shirt box, or on poster board.
3. **Game directions.** Cut out the game directions (below) and glue them to the front of the file folder, on the outside of the shirt box, or on the edge of the poster board.
4. **Two game title labels.** Glue one game title label to the file folder tab, on the outside of the shirt box, or on the poster board, and then laminate for durability.
5. **Self-sealing plastic storage bag.** Tape the second game title label on the self-sealing plastic bag and then staple or tape the bag to the front of the file folder, top of the shirt box, or on the edge of the poster board.
6. **Game cards.** Cut out the game cards found on page 107 and laminate for durability. Place the cards in the self-sealing plastic bag. Your game is now ready to play!

Game Objective: The objective is for the child to correctly place the gumball game cards (with pictures representing phonemes /d/ /h/ /n/ /w/ /z/) on the gumball machine that has the picture with the "same" beginning sound.

To Play the Game: Place the game cards in a pile face-up. The child draws the top card, says the name of the item pictured on the gumball card, and then places the card on the gumball machine that has a picture that begins with the same sound.

To Modify the Game for Struggling Learners: For children struggling with learning how to identify beginning sounds, use only half the game board. The children will only have to choose between two different beginning sounds.

Self-Checking: On the back of each of the gumball game cards is the picture on the gumball machine that has the same beginning sound.

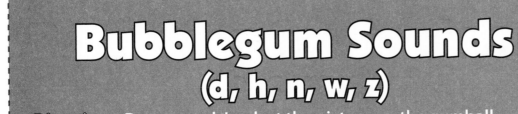

Bubblegum Sounds
(d, h, n, w, z)

Directions: Draw a card. Look at the picture on the gumball. Say its name.

Find the gumball machine with a picture that starts with the same sound. Put it in the matching gumball machine.

Bubblegum Sounds

Bubblegum Sounds

(This page was purposely left blank.)

Bubblegum

(This page was purposely left blank.)

Sounds

(This page was purposely left blank.)

**Beginning
Sound
Picture Key:**

"W" Pictures:
watch, window, wolf

"N" Pictures:
nest, needle, net

"Z" Pictures:
zipper, zero, zucchini

"D" Pictures:
desk, duck, dog

"H" Pictures:
horse, hammer, hose

Game 13:
First Sound Flags

Skill: Matching initial sound pictures (j, k, p, r, v)

Preparation and Assembly

1. **Remove the game materials.** Carefully remove the "First Sound Flags" game materials found on pages 109–116.
2. **Make the game board.** Glue the two folder game pages (pages 111 and 113) to the inside of a file folder, shirt box, or on poster board.
3. **Game directions.** Cut out the game directions (below) and glue them to the front of the file folder, on the outside of the shirt box, or on the edge of the poster board.
4. **Two game title labels.** Glue one game title label to the file folder tab, on the outside of the shirt box, or on the poster board, and then laminate for durability.

5. **Self-sealing plastic storage bag.** Tape the second game title label on the self-sealing plastic bag and then staple or tape the bag to the front of the file folder, top of the shirt box, or on the edge of the poster board.
6. **Game cards.** Cut out the game cards found on page 115 and laminate for durability. Place the cards in the self-sealing plastic bag. Your game is now ready to play!

Game Objective: The objective is for the child to correctly place the flag game cards (with pictures representing phonemes /j/ /k/ /p/ /r/ /v/) on the flagpoles that have the picture with the "same" beginning sound.

To Play the Game: Place the flag game cards in a pile face-up. The child draws the top card, says the name of the item pictured on the flag game card, and then places the card on the flagpole that has a picture that begins with the same sound.

To Modify the Game for Struggling Learners: Play this game with the child who is struggling with learning how to identify beginning sounds. Pick up a flag card and slowly say the name of the picture, emphasizing the beginning sound. Then, say the beginning sound in isolation. Next, in the same way you said the name of the picture on the card, say the name of the pictures on each of the flagpoles. Then decide together on which flagpole the child should place the flag.

Self-Checking: On the back of each of the flag game cards is the picture on the flagpole that has the same beginning sound.

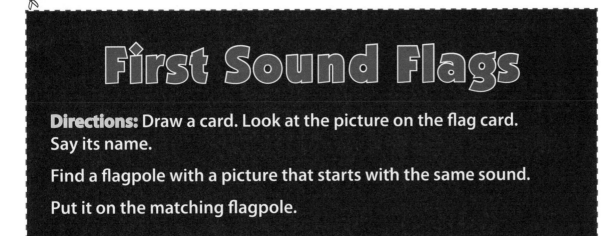

First Sound Flags

Directions: Draw a card. Look at the picture on the flag card. Say its name.

Find a flagpole with a picture that starts with the same sound.

Put it on the matching flagpole.

First Sound Flags

First Sound Flags

(This page was purposely left blank.)

First Sound Flags

(First Sound Flags Folder Left-Side)

(This page was purposely left blank.)

(This page was purposely left blank.)

Beginning Sound Picture Key:
Rabbit Flagpole: rhinoceros, rocket
Van Flagpole: vegetables, vase
Pig Flagpole: penguin, panda
Jar Flagpole: jam, Jack-in-the-box
King Flagpole: key, koala

Game 14:
Scooping Sounds

Skill: Matching initial sound pictures to letters (b, c, m, s)

Preparation and Assembly

1. **Remove the game materials.** Carefully remove the "Scooping Sounds" game materials found on pages 117–126.
2. **Make the game board.** Glue the two folder game pages (pages 119 and 121) to the inside of a file folder, shirt box, or on poster board.
3. **Game directions.** Cut out the game directions (below) and glue them to the front of the file folder, on the outside of the shirt box, or on the edge of the poster board.
4. **Two game title labels.** Glue one game title label to the file folder tab, on the outside of the shirt box, or on the poster board, and then laminate for durability.

5. **Self-sealing plastic storage bag.** Tape the second game title label on the self-sealing plastic bag and then staple or tape the bag to the front of the file folder, top of the shirt box, or on the edge of the poster board.
6. **Game cards.** Cut out the game cards found on pages123 and 125 and laminate for durability. Place the cards in the self-sealing plastic bag. Your game is now ready to play!

Game Objective: The objective is for the child to correctly make a three-scoop ice cream cone by finding three ice cream scoops with pictures that start with the same sound as the letter on the ice cream cone.

To Play the Game: Place the ice cream scoop game cards in a pile face-up. The child draws the top card, says the name of the picture on the ice cream scoop game card, and then places the ice cream scoop card on top of the cone that has the letter that is the same beginning sound as the ice cream scoop picture.

To Modify the Game for Struggling Learners: First, make sure that the child can identify the letters on the cones and is able to say the sound of each of those letters. For children struggling with learning how to identify beginning sounds, use only half of the game board and half of the game cards. The children will only have to choose between two different beginning sounds.

Self-Checking: On the back of each of the ice cream scoop game cards is the letter of the cone that has the same beginning sound.

Scooping Sounds
(b, c, m, s)

Directions: Look at the picture on the ice cream scoop card. Say its name.

Find an ice cream cone with the letter that has the same matching sound. Put it on top of the matching cone.

Scooping Sounds

Scooping Sounds

(This page was purposely left blank.)

(Scooping Sounds Folder Left-Side)

-119-

(This page was purposely left blank.)

Sounds

(Scooping Sounds Folder Right-Side)

(This page was purposely left blank.)

Beginning Sound Picture Key: **"B" Cone:** bee, balloons, banana
"M" Cone: monkey, mask, milk

B

B

-124-

Beginning Sound Picture Key: **"C" Cone:** cow, corn, cat
"S" Cone: soap, seal, scissors

Game 15:
Four Sound Circus

Skill: Matching initial sound pictures to letters (f, g, l, t)

Preparation and Assembly

1. **Remove the game materials.** Carefully remove the "Four Sound CIrcus" game materials found on pages 127–134.
2. **Make the game board.** Glue the two folder game pages (pages 129 and 131) to the inside of a file folder, shirt box, or on poster board.
3. **Game directions.** Cut out the game directions (below) and glue them to the front of the file folder, on the outside of the shirt box, or on the edge of the poster board.
4. **Two game title labels.** Glue one game title label to the file folder tab, on the outside of the shirt box, or on the poster board, and then laminate for durability.
5. **Self-sealing plastic storage bag.** Tape the second game title label on the self-sealing plastic bag and then staple or tape the bag to the front of the file folder, top of the shirt box, or on the edge of the poster board.
6. **Game cards.** Cut out the game cards found on page 133 and laminate for durability. Place the cards in the self-sealing plastic bag. Your game is now ready to play!

Game Objective: The objective is for the child to correctly place three circus dogs in each of the circus rings by matching the beginning sound on the dog's ball to the beginning letter sound above each circus ring.

To Play the Game: Place the circus dog game cards in a pile face-up. The child draws the top card, says the name of the picture on the circus dog game card, and then places the card in the circus ring that has the letter that has the same beginning sound as the picture on the circus dog's ball.

To Modify the Game for Struggling Learners: First, make sure that the child can identify the letters on the curtains and is able to say the sound each of the letters represents. For children struggling with learning how to identify beginning sounds, use only half the game board and half the game cards. The children will only have to choose between two different beginning sounds.

Self-Checking: On the back of each of the circus dog game cards is the letter of the circus that has the same beginning sound.

Four Sound Circus
(f, g, l, t)

Directions: Draw a card. Look at the picture on the circus dog card. Say its name.

Find the circus ring with the letter that has the same matching sound. Put the card on the correct space in the matching circus ring.

Four Sound Circus

Four Sound Circus

(This page was purposely left blank.)

(Four Sound Circus Folder Left-Side)

(This page was purposely left blank.)

(Four Sound Circus Folder Right-Side)

(This page was purposely left blank.)

Beginning Sound Picture Key:
"T" Ring: turtle, tomato, tent

"F" Ring:
fork, fish, fan

"L" Ring:
ladybug, lemon, leaf

"G" Ring:
guitar, girl, gift

(Four Sounds Circus Cards)

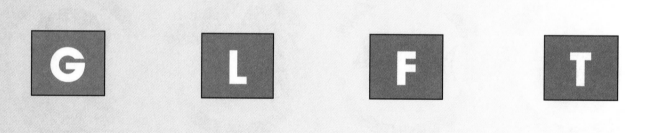

Fill the Nests

Skill: Matching initial sound pictures to letters (d, h, n, w, z)

Preparation and Assembly

1. **Remove the game materials.** Carefully remove the "Fill the Nests" game materials found on pages 135–142.
2. **Make the game board.** Glue the two folder game pages (pages 137 and 139) to the inside of a file folder, shirt box, or on poster board.
3. **Game directions.** Cut out the game directions (below) and glue them to the front of the file folder, on the outside of the shirt box, or on the edge of the poster board.
4. **Two game title labels.** Glue one game title label to the file folder tab, on the outside of the shirt box, or on the poster board, and then laminate for durability.
5. **Self-sealing plastic storage bag.** Tape the second game title label on the self-sealing plastic bag and then staple or tape the bag to the front of the file folder, top of the shirt box, or on the edge of the poster board.
6. **Game cards.** Cut out the game cards found on page 141 and laminate for durability. Place the cards in the self-sealing plastic bag. Your game is now ready to play!

Game Objective: The objective is for the child to correctly place three eggs in each of the five bird nests by matching the beginning sound from the picture on each egg to the beginning letter sound displayed on the nests.

To Play the Game: Place the egg game cards in a pile face-up. The child draws the top card, says the name of the picture on the egg game card, and then places the card in the nest that has the letter with the same beginning sound as the picture on the egg card.

To Modify the Game for Struggling Learners: First, make sure that the child can identify the letters on the nests and is able to say the sound each of the letters represents. For children struggling with learning how to identify beginning sounds, use only half the game board and half the game cards. The children will only have to choose between two different beginning sounds.

Self-Checking: On the back of each of the egg game cards is the letter of the nest that has the same beginning sound.

Fill the Nests
(d, h, n, w, z)

Directions: Draw a card. Look at the picture on the egg. Say its name.

Find a nest with a letter that has the same sound as the picture.

Put the egg card in the nest with the matching sound.

Fill the Nests

Fill the Nests

(This page was purposely left blank.)

(Fill the Nests Folder Left-Side)

(This page was purposely left blank.)

(Fill the Nests Folder Right-Side)

(This page was purposely left blank.)

Beginning Sound Picture Key: **"N" Nest:** nine, nail, nut **"H" Nest:** hat, hose, helicopter
"W" Nest: walrus, wagon, watermelon **"D" Nest:** doll, dog, deer **"Z" Nest:** zipper, zucchini, zebra

(Fill the Nests Cards)

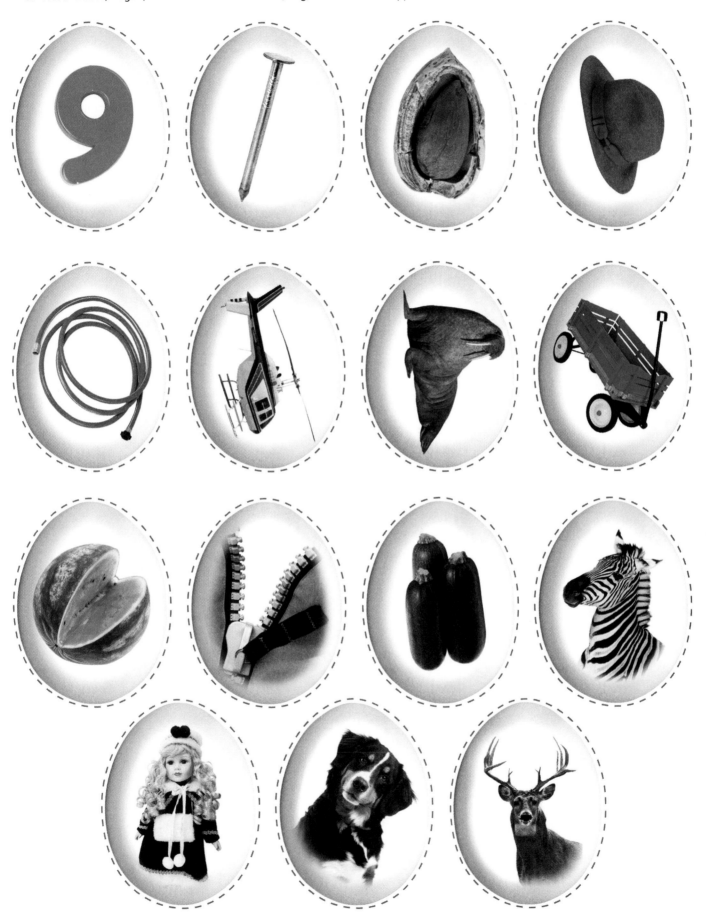

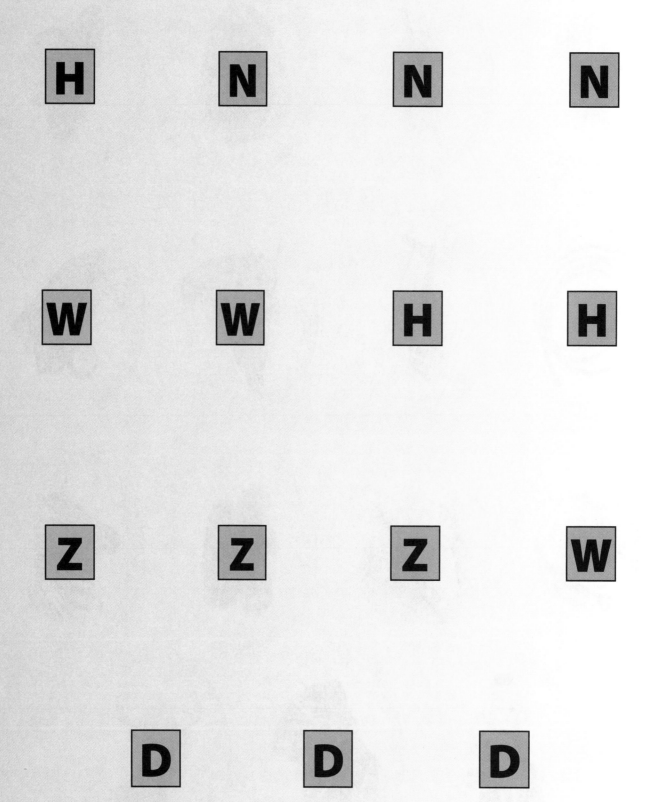

Game 17:
Sound Shelves

Skill: Matching initial sound pictures to letters (j, k, p, r, v)

Preparation and Assembly

1. **Remove the game materials.** Carefully remove the "Sound Shelves" game materials found on pages 143–150.

2. **Make the game board.** Glue the two folder game pages (pages 145 and 147) to the inside of a file folder, shirt box, or on poster board.

3. **Game directions.** Cut out the game directions (below) and glue them to the front of the file folder, on the outside of the shirt box, or on the edge of the poster board.

4. **Two game title labels.** Glue one game title label to the file folder tab, on the outside of the shirt box, or on the poster board, and then laminate for durability.

5. **Self-sealing plastic storage bag.** Tape the second game title label on the self-sealing plastic bag and then staple or tape the bag to the front of the file folder, top of the shirt box, or on the edge of the poster board.

6. **Game cards.** Cut out the game cards found on page 149 and laminate for durability. Place the cards in the self-sealing plastic bag. Your game is now ready to play!

Game Objective: The objective is for the child to correctly place three books on each of the five book shelves by matching the beginning sound on the book to the beginning letter sound on each shelf.

To Play the Game: Place the book game cards in a pile face-up. The child draws the top card, says the name of the picture on the book game card, and then places the card on the book shelf that has the letter that has the same beginning sound as the picture on the book.

To Modify the Game for Struggling Learners: First, make sure that the child can identify the letters on the shelves and is able to say the sound each of the letters represents. For children struggling with learning how to identify beginning sounds, use only half the game board and half the game cards. The children will only have to choose between two different beginning sounds.

Self-Checking: On the back of each of the book game cards is the letter of the shelf that has the same beginning sound.

Sound Shelves
(j, k, p, r, v)

Directions: Draw a card. Look at the picture on the book. Say its name.

Find a shelf with a letter that has the same sound as the picture.

Put the book card on the shelf with the matching sound.

Sound Shelves | Sound Shelves

Sound Shelves | Sound Shelves

(This page was purposely left blank.)

j, k, p, r, v
Sound Shelves

"r" shelf

"j" shelf

(Sound Shelves Folder Left-Side)

(This page was purposely left blank.)

"v" shelf

"k" shelf

"p" shelf

(Sound Shelves Folder Right-Side)

(This page was purposely left blank.)

(Sound Shelves Cards)

Beginning Sound Picture Key:
"J" Nest: jet, jacket, jellybeans
"K" Nest: kite, key, kangaroo
"P" Nest: pillow, pizza, paint
"R" Nest: rake, ring, rainbow
"V" Nest: violin, vest, vase

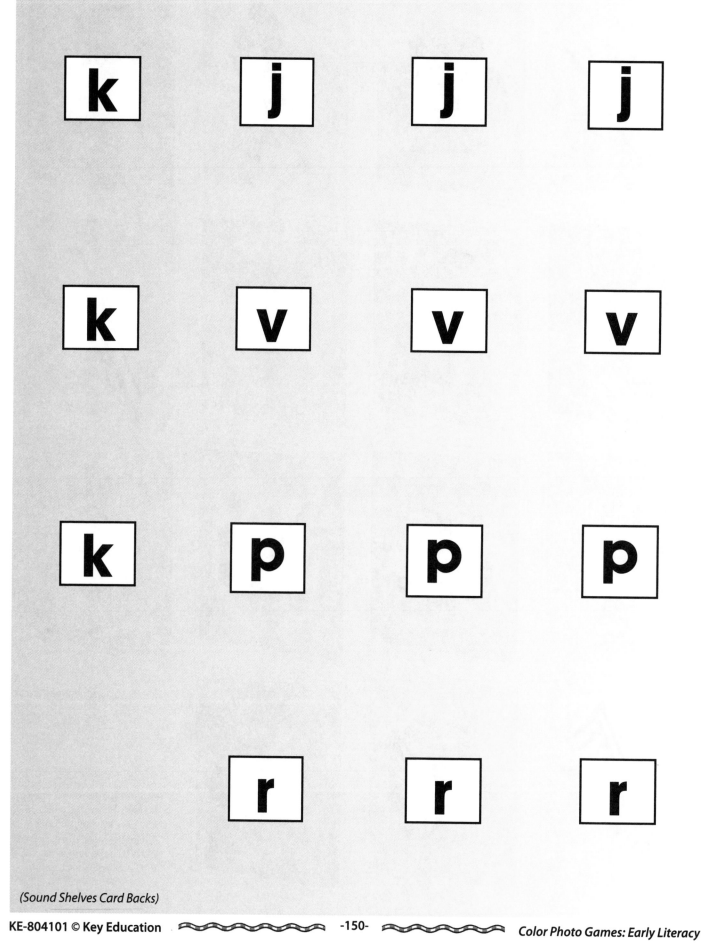

(Sound Shelves Card Backs)

Game 18:
Alphabet Train (A-Z)

Skill: Alphabetical order – match letters to pictures

Preparation and Assembly

1. **Remove the game materials.** Carefully remove the "Alphabet Train (A –Z)" game materials found on pages 151–160.
2. **Make the game board.** Glue the two folder game pages (pages 153 and 155) to the inside of a file folder, shirt box, or on poster board.
3. **Game directions.** Cut out the game directions (below) and glue them to the front of the file folder, on the outside of the shirt box, or on the edge of the poster board.
4. **Two game title labels.** Glue one game title label to the file folder tab, on the outside of the shirt box, or on the poster board, and then laminate for durability.
5. **Self-sealing plastic storage bag.** Tape the second game title label on the self-sealing plastic bag and then staple or tape the bag to the front of the file folder, top of the shirt box, or on the edge of the poster board.
6. **Game cards.** Cut out the game cards found on pages 157 and 159 and laminate for durability. Place the cards in the self-sealing plastic bag. Your game is now ready to play!

Game Objective: The objective is for the child to correctly place all the train cars in alphabetical order.

To Play the Game: Place the train car game cards in a scattered pile face-up. The child should sort the cards and line them up alphabetically behind the train engine.

To Modify the Game for Struggling Learners: First, make sure that the child can identify the letters on the train cars. Sort the cards into alphabetical groups of 3 or 4 cards. For example, sort the cards into the group A, B, C, and D. The next group would be E, F, G, and H. Give the child only a few cards at a time to put in order.

Self-Checking: On the back of each train car game card is a number. The number corresponds to the letters placement in the alphabet; for example, "A" is number "1" and "Z" is number "26." When the child completes the alphabet train, he can turn over the cards to see if he is correct. If he is correct, the cards will be in numerical order from 1 to 26.

Alphabet Train (A-Z)

Directions: Look at the letters on the train cars.

Say the name of each letter.

Place the train cars in alphabetical order.

Alphabet Train

Alphabet Train

(This page was purposely left blank.)

(This page was purposely left blank.)

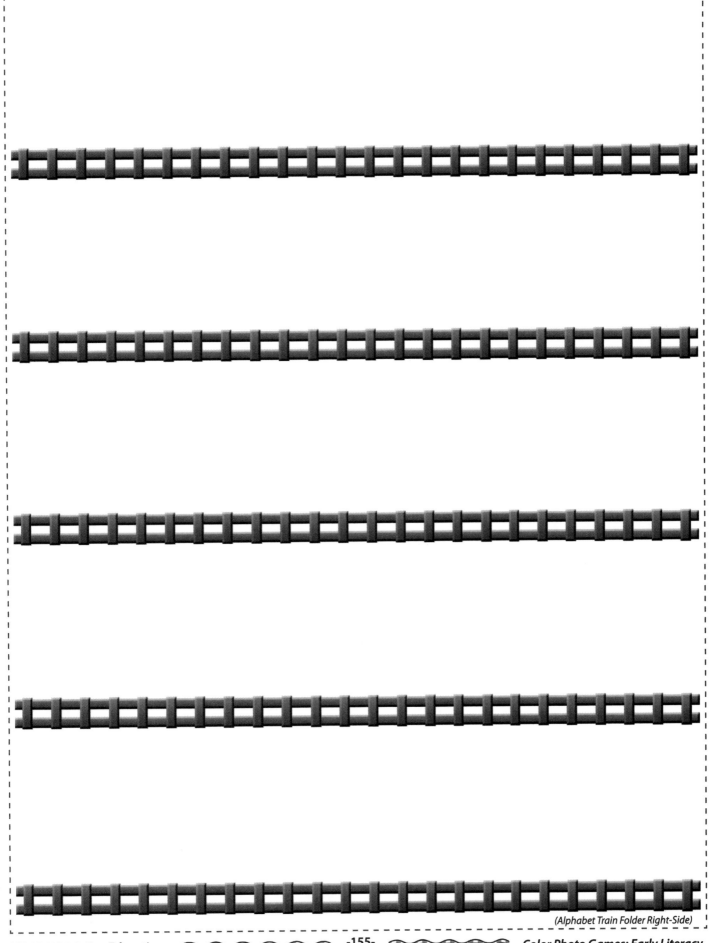

(Alphabet Train Folder Right-Side)

(This page was purposely left blank.)

Beginning Sound Picture Key: **A**-apple **B**-banana **C**-car **D**-dog **E**-elephant
F-fox **G**-goat **H**-hat **I**-igloo **J**-jar **K**-key **L**-lion **M**-mask **N**-nest **O**-octopus

3	2	1
6	5	4
9	8	7
12	11	10
15	14	13

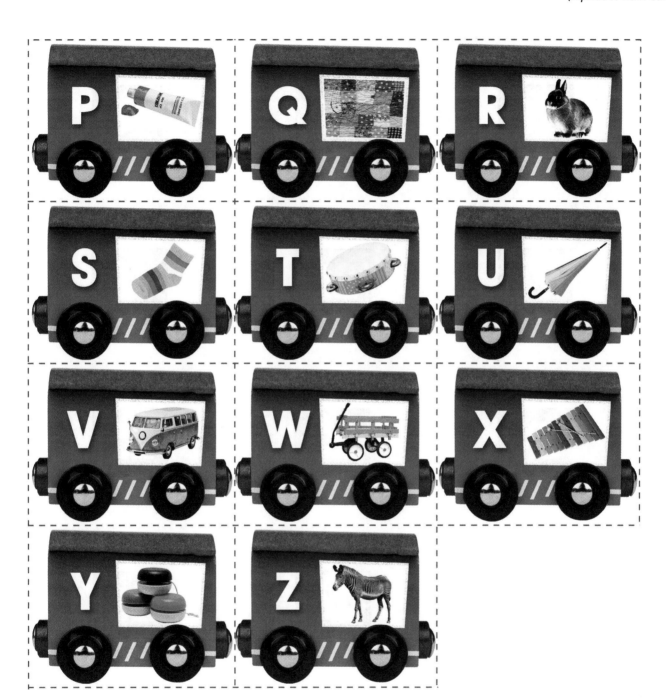

Beginning Sound Picture Key:

P-paint	**V**-van
Q-quilt	**W**-wagon
R-rabbit	**X**-xylophone
S-sock	**Y**-yo-yos
T-tambourine	**Z**-zebra
U-umbrella	

18	17	16
21	20	19
24	23	22
	26	25